MODERN INTERIORS
DESIGNSOURCE

MODERN INTERIORS DESIGNSOURCE

COLLINS DESIGN
An Imprint of HarperCollins Publishers

MODERN INTERIORS DESIGNSOURCE
Copyright © 2007 COLLINS Design and LOFT Publications

First Edition published in 2007 by:
Collins Design
An Imprint of HarperCollins*Publishers*
10 East 53rd Street
New York, NY 10022
Tel.: (212) 207-7000
Fax: (212) 207-7654
collinsdesign@harpercollins.com
www.harpercollins.com

Distributed throughout the world by:
HarperCollins*Publishers*
10 East 53rd Street
New York, NY 10022
Fax: (212) 207-7654

Packaged by:
LOFT Publications
Via Laietana, 32 4.° Of. 92
08003 Barcelona, Spain
Tel.: +34 932 688 088
Fax: +34 932 687 073
loft@loftpublications.com
www.loftpublications.com

Editor and texts:
Bridget Vranckx

Art Director:
Mireia Casanovas Soley

Layout:
Anabel Naranjo

Library of Congress Control Number: 2007926715

ISBN: 978-0-06-124202-1

Printed by:
Artes Gráficas Toledo - Mondadori Printing
/ Pozzoni Group, Spain

Third Printing, 2010

Introduction

Residences in the twenty-first century reflect the luxury of expanding choices and the constraints of diminishing horizons. Advances in design and technology let us choose virtually whatever style makes us feel at home. Some houses mirror what we imagined as futuristic only a few decades ago, while others cling to the warmth of a bygone era, blending the past with contemporary materials, and technologies. At the same time, we continue to need space and light and natural surroundings. But in today's world, available building space is shrinking and so is nearby green space. More and more, we expect interiors to provide the solution. Designers and architects these days are learning how to get the most out of a house's footprint with large, unencumbered spaces that multitask. And they are bringing us closer to nature and light. Their common goal: flexibility and a close interior-exterior relationship. The following pages present some of the latest and most interesting solutions to modern needs, shaped by our desire to express a personal style. All are achieved through interior design, the focus of this volume.

Interior styles should be a direct reflection of who we are. To achieve this, interior designers have to be creative, often marrying modern techniques, methods, or ideas with styles of the past, such as Arts and Crafts or mid-twentieth-century modern. We also want our homes to be sanctuaries where we can escape the overload of contemporary societies. At the same time, globalization has opened us up to diverse creative influences. Paradoxically, globalization has also deliv-

ered a certain type of homogeneity, and people are struggling to preserve their individuality. In the process, they seem to be ever-more introverted.

One of society's major predicaments is the lack of space, both land for construction and room inside existing homes. Designers have responded with innovative techniques and solutions to turn homes into flexible spaces. Many contemporary homes are modeled on the loft concept to fill the current need for ease of movement. In many cases, interiors have been stripped of unnecessary doors and walls to reveal roomy open spaces—perhaps in reaction to the claustrophobic situation in society at large. Designers today work with partitions and color, levels, and versatile furniture; and they employ practical materials, such as concrete, glass, and wood, to differentiate traditional functional areas.

As space diminishes, so does light, and designers are working to incorporate more of this essential element. Though we are increasingly becoming introverted, we will always reach out to nature—albeit from the comfort of our homes—wanting to be part of it as the space around us disappears and communities become ever denser. New homes are being designed with glass walls, clerestories and other amenities to ensure that maximum sunlight reaches the interior. Existing buildings, in parallel, are being updated so that once-dark spaces can be flooded with daylight, opening up the inside to the outside.

These are some of the ways interior designers are helping us live with the challenges of today's world. Look inside. You might find the design solution you've been looking for.

Pied-à-terre | Pablo Uribe/Studio Uribe

Location: Miami Beach, FL, USA | Photos © Claudia Uribe

All the interior walls of this second home were eliminated to gain space. This home is the essence of simplicity: colors are bright and light, and there are few extraneous adornments.

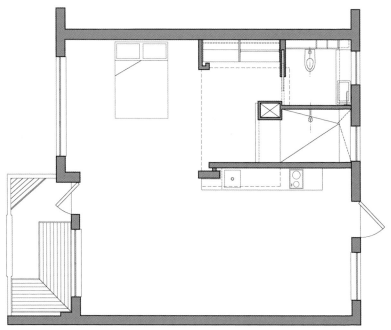

Floor plan

The bed is placed opposite the sofa to create a feeling of continuity and make the space feel larger than it is. The kitchen is located inside the entrance hall, next to the dining area.

Polished cement floors and aluminum windows
lend simplicity and elegance to this home, which
is used sporadically by its owners—for example,
after a day at the beach or after concerts.

Roszak House | Thomas Roszak

Location: Chicago, IL, USA | Photos © Jon Millar, Hedrich Blessing

The design for this house in the suburbs centers on a 16-by-16-foot structural module—the size of all the rooms. The exceptions are the living room and garage, each of which measure 24.3 by 32.6 feet.

Ground floor

First floor

The use of concrete, metal and glass throughout the building, give this home an essentially modern feeling, underlined by a computer system that controls many of the functions in the house.

Home in Vilada | Agustí Costa, Estudi de Disseny

Location: Vilada, Spain | Photos © David Cardelús

Among the main aims for this country home was to achieve substantial interaction between the interior and the exterior, and to make the interior fluid so as to flood it with natural light. Cool, light colors and materials predominate

First floor

Longitudinal section

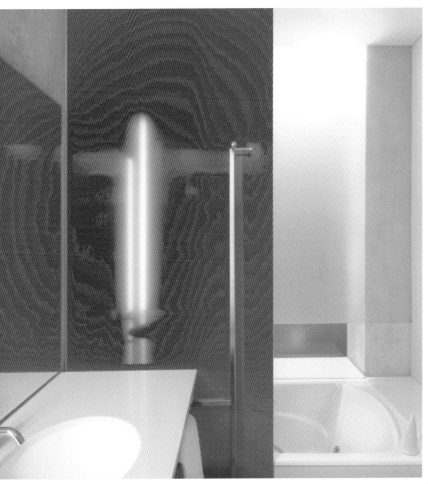

The interior design of this home in the country uses modern materials and technologies, including wooden floors, iron bookshelves, and exposed thermo-clay walls.

A false backlit Corian ceiling adds a touch of warmth to the bedrooms and main bathroom. The furniture is minimal and has been designed to suit the space.

The large thermo-clay wall continues uninterrupted throughout the home. Not even the staircase disrupts its continuity, as the steps are inserted without beams.

Ground floor

Garden level

Vineyard Residence | John Wardle Architects

Location: Mornington Peninsula, Victoria, Australia | Photos © Trevor Mein

Set within a large vineyard, this 4,300-square-foot residence responds to the ordered patterns of the grapevine rows as well as to the expansive views across the surrounding farmland.

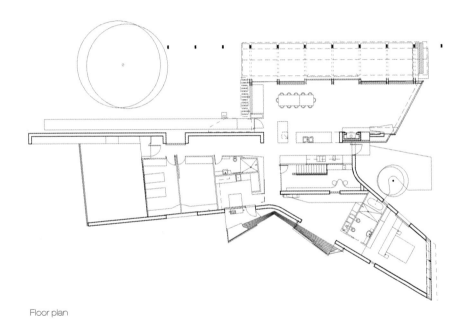

Floor plan

The palette of materials—heavy timber framing
and slim steelwork—sits comfortably in this rural
setting, and the large, light-filled interior commu-
nicates with the exterior.

Summerhouse | Peter Hulting/Meter Arkitektur

Location: Gothenburg, Sweden | Photos © James Silverman

To create more space in this 538-square-foot summerhouse on the west coast of Sweden, the architect found compact solutions for sleeping, storing, bathing, eating, and cooking.

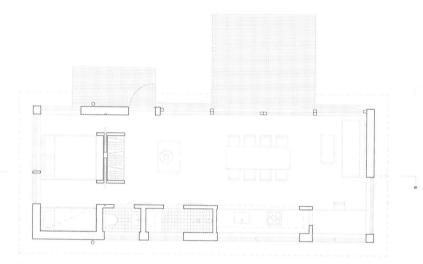

Floor plan

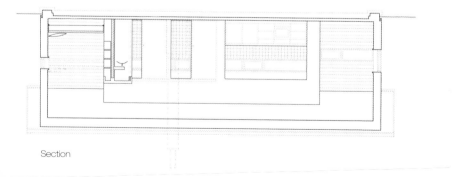

Section

Isolated House | Marià Castelló Martínez

Location: Formentera, Spain | Photos © Jordi Canosa

This north-south facing volume incorporates both living quarters and a small architecture practice. A service area at the core of the structure bisects the private and work areas.

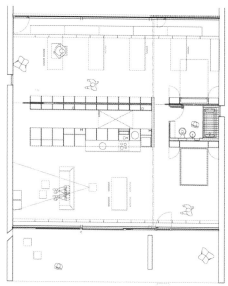

Floor plan

Hiller Residence | Michael P. Johnson Design Studios

Location: Winter Park, CO, USA | Photos © Bill Timmerman

Like being in a fishbowl in the middle of the woods, the main room on the lower level with the suspended fireplace is an incredibly cozy room thanks also to solar gain through the windows and in-floor radiant heating.

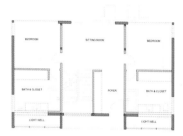

Lower level

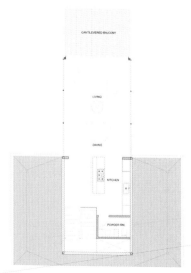

Upper level

The incredible openness of this house—achieved by using few doors, a light color scheme, minimal furniture, and as many openings towards the exterior as possible—creates a relaxing environment.

The staircase's wooden steps seem to float up and down the levels, connecting the upstairs and downstairs without intruding into the living space.

Wheatsheaf House | Jesse Judd Architects

Location: Wheatsheaf, South Australia, Australia | Photos © Peter Bennetts

To minimize the impact on the environment, this house was slightly raised from the ground and rests on piles. The deep red color inside lends a warm ambience to this second home.

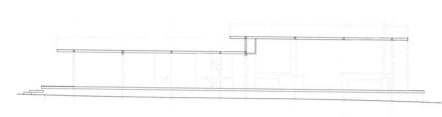

Longitudinal section

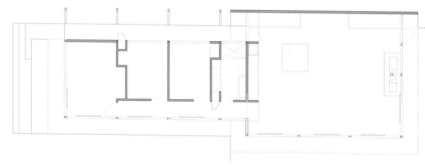

Floor plan

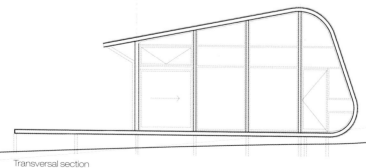

Transversal section

The living area is separated from the bedrooms. The house is completely open to the dense eucalyptus forest outside, which creates a special relationship between the interior and exterior.

Dok | Querkraft Architekten

Location: Vienna, Austria | Photos © Hertha Hurnaus

Only light colors—white and gray—are used throughout to reflect the sparse sunlight of the northern slope on which these identical homes are situated. Window walls and massive skylights give sunlight direct access.

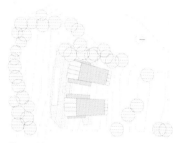

Ground floor

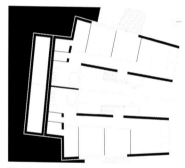

First floor

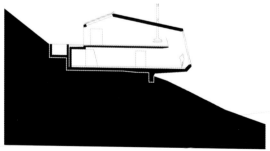

Section

Single Family House | Josep Ma. Esquius Prat

Location: St. Fruitós de Bages, Spain | Photos © Lourdes Jansana

This family home is divided over three levels. The majority of the rooms are on the first floor. The parents' area is on the top floor with a garage on the ground level.

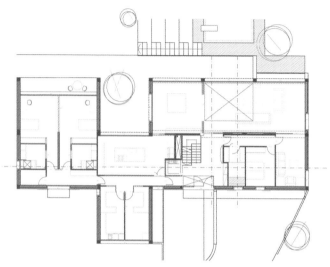

Ground floor

Section

White predomintes inside this home, with the exception of the stuccoed alfresco mural near the staircase. The white walls set off the tobacco-colored wood flooring.

In the bathroom, the dark brown flooring contrasts with the glass doors and mosaic tiling, creating a very elegant room and a calm and relaxed ambience.

The Ariav House | Alex Meitlis Architecture & Design

Location: Tel Aviv, Israel | Photos © Yael Pincus

This house in the suburbs south of Tel Aviv is located in the center of the plot surrounded by a large garden. The narrow residence measures 19 feet wide and 103 feet long.

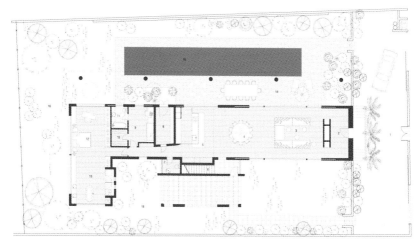

Ground floor

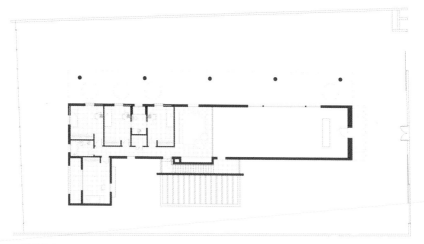

First floor

The entire house, inside and out, was designed by Alex Meitlis Architecture & Design. The firm used transparent elements throughout to create the feeling of a space without boundaries.

Windows are placed on both sides of the narrow living room and the master bedroom and bath so the surrounding garden can be enjoyed from these two principal areas of the house.

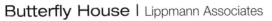

Butterfly House | Lippmann Associates

Location: Sydney, New South Wales, Australia | Photos © Willem Rethmeier

This house on Sydney's rocky coastline, Dover Heights, has few straight lines and is designed according to Feng Shui principles.

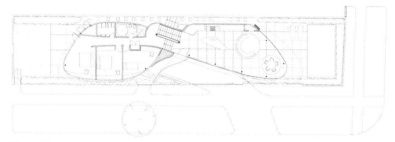

Ground floor

First floor

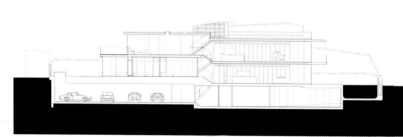

Longitudinal section

The layout is divided into east and west wings, and the project also uses two floors to differentiate the areas. A mesh of metal columns protrudes to create balconies.

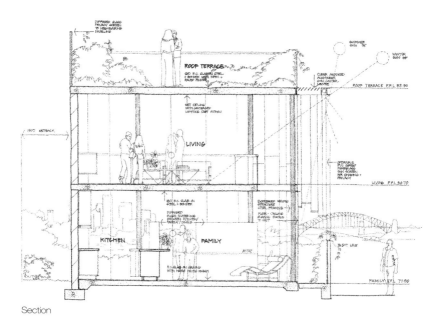

Section

The exterior walls are made of glass, affording the inhabitants fantastic views over the ocean, the nearby cliffs, Sydney Bay, Harbor Bridge, and the famous Opera House.

The morning sun floods the bedrooms, which are in the east wing of the house, while the living room—in the west wing—basks in the glow of the sunsets.

Silverman Residence | Michael P. Johnson Design Studios

Location: Scottsdale, AZ, USA | Photos © Bill Timmerman

As in other Michael P. Johnson houses, glass walls, partitions, and furniture make the spaces feel fluid and unencumbered.

Lower level

Upper level

This house, enclosed by 26 feet high walls, is built on a restricted site, in the middle of a residential block. A structural concrete nucleus passes through the interior and shapes the living room.

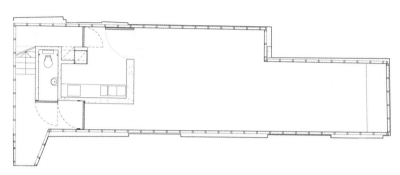

Ground floor

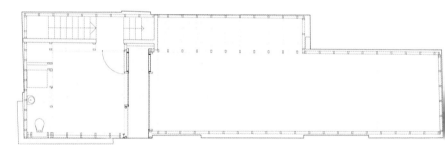

First floor

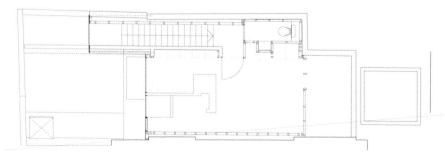

Second floor

A special setting treatment for the concrete gives this basic material a smoother and shinier appearance and enhances the rooms with an organic and tactile dimension.

The house is organized around three areas: the living room on the ground floor, the guest bedroom on the first floor, and the master bedroom suite with bathroom and terrace on the top floor.

Yarra Bend House | John Wardle Architects

Location: Melbourne, Victoria, Australia | Photos © Trevor Mein

This house for a family of four, located on a steeply sloping site that drops away to the Yarra River below, has a surprising spatially rich interior.

Ground floor

First floor

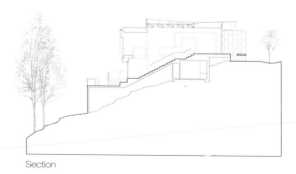

Section

An unusual skylight, using a precise, inventive geometry, enlivens the space above the central staircase with a diffusion of the incoming light and a play of shadows.

The house enjoys spectacular views from all sides. A subtle interplay of volume, compression, and expansion creates varying degrees of seclusion in each area of the residence.

A central volume made of bamboo and MDF painted in white integrates the kitchen and bathroom functions as well as storage space, leaving the rest of the house free to develop around it.

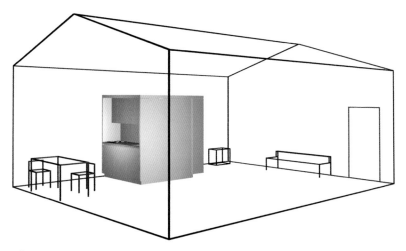

Perspective

The bathroom surfaces have been covered in polyester of an intense epoxi green. None of the doors of this volume have handles.

Every part of this small custom-built house exudes mathematical precision. To maintain visual spaciousness, only the minimalist stairway separates the kitchen from the living room.

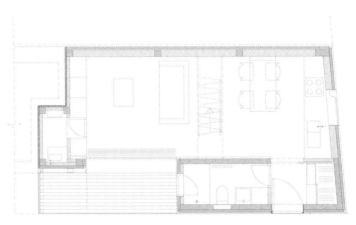

Ground floor

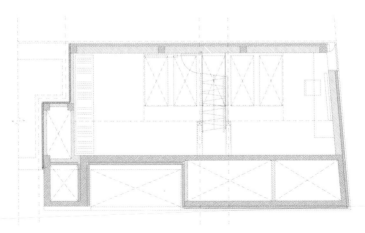

First floor

After careful study of the available light in this north-facing house, a skylight was built in the roof to allow daylight to reach the ground floor via the stairwell.

Despite its extra-extra-small dimensions, this house feels much bigger than it actually is, thanks to the fluidity, openness, and simplicity of the spaces.

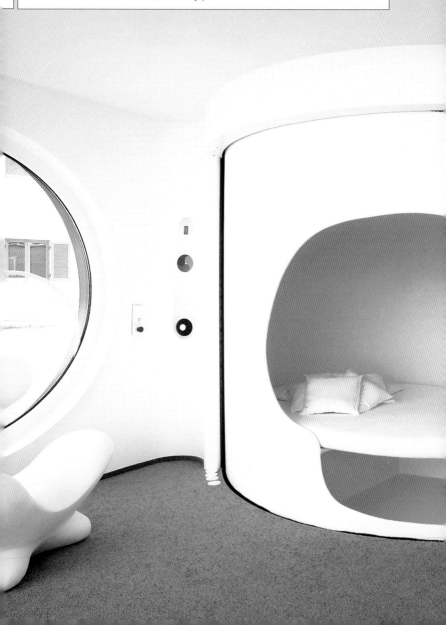

A space-saving rotating drum placed in one corner of this 387.5 square-foot wooden box holds the kitchen, bedroom, and bathroom and can be moved into position as needed to optimize domestic space.

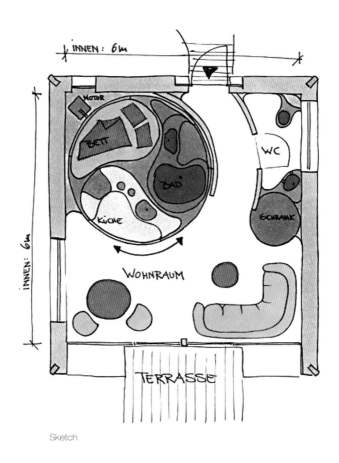

Sketch

With its molded, organically shaped plastic elements, the rotor house has a very futuristic feel, yet its compact functionality is not far from the growing needs of a number city dwellers around the world.

City Hill House | John Wardle Architects

Location: Melbourne, Victoria, Australia | Photos © Trevor Mein

The house is on an elevated site, with commanding views of the city to the northwest. A two-story-high wall is the defining feature of the interior.

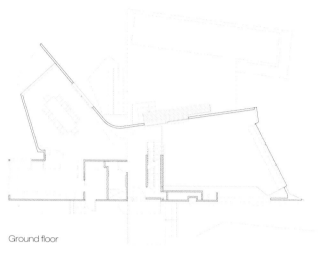

Ground floor

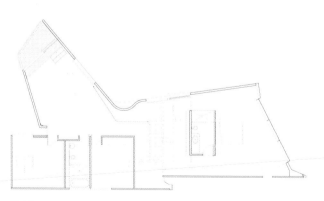

First floor

Idiosyncratic bends in the floor plan crimp the spaces at particular points to taper views to a slice. The views are revealed as the spaces expand.

H House | Archikubik

Location: Sant Andreu de Llavaneres, Spain | Photos © Miquel Tres

H is for honesty and for the shape of the house, say the architects. The parents' space was placed in one volume on the east side and the daughter's space in the other volume, on the west side.

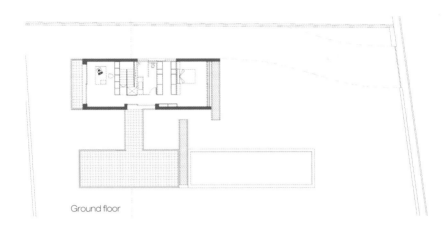

Ground floor

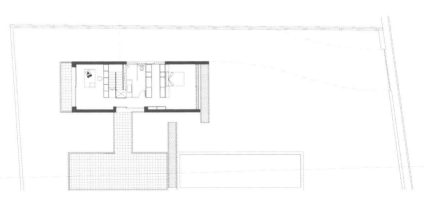

First floor

This house has no doors or hallways (except in the entrance hall). The use of three colors throughout endows the home with visual continuity and a feeling of modernity.

Downing Residence | Chiba Ibarra Rosano Design

Location: Tucson, AZ, USA | Photos © Bill Timmerman

This spacious house in Arizona consists of three pavilions that are connected by a glass passageway. One of the volumes houses the living room, dining room, and kitchen on the ground floor.

Floor plan

A number of panels and partitions divide this two-bedroom apartment into individual functional areas. A glass wall, inside a deep frame, separates the dining area from the living room.

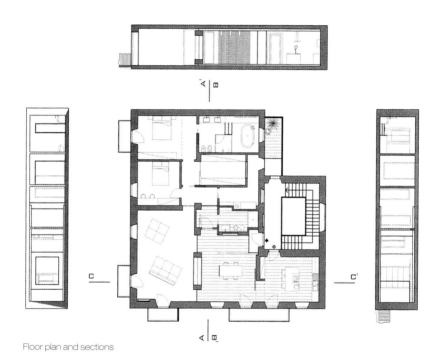

Floor plan and sections

The shower is separated from the raised bathing area by glass walls. Transparency, light, and mutual tones are fundamental interior design elements of this loft.

A sophisticated, modern effect is achieved in this two-bedroom home which uses a lot of white, touches of wood, light brown colors, and some aluminum.

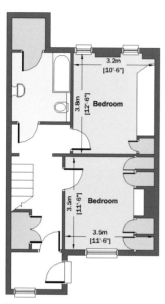

Lower ground floor

Ground floor

First floor

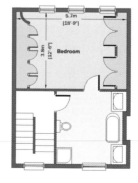

Second floor

Third floor

The large open reception area is located next to the kitchen. The pure white walls interspersed with black corners, set off the caramel-colored parquet flooring and give this home a warm touch.

The modern all-white cinema-cum-studio on the top floor and the white bathroom below it are in stark contrast to the wood-paneled wall and subtle lighting of the bedroom, which give them a romantic, timeless appeal.

A huge flat-screen television and loudspeakers are incorporated into the wall. The aluminum and glass workspace tucked in the corner is unobtrusive in this all-white room.

Nomad Home | Gerold Peham

Location: Salzburg, Austria | Photos © Nomad Home® Trading GesmbH

This transportable home represents spatial efficiency and geographical flexibility. Simple and ingenious, the construction resembles that of a modular nomad home system.

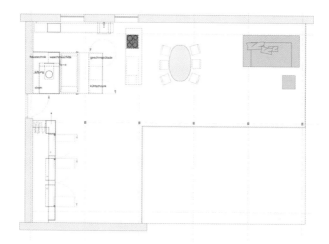

Floor plan

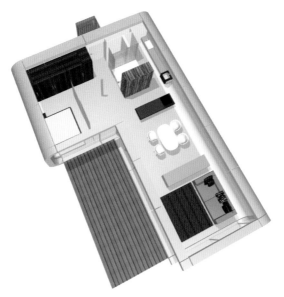

Render

The nomad home's specially designed furniture ensures optimum use of available space. The kitchen unit and wall closet are extremely functional and provide additional storage space.

The kitchen unit acts as a divider, separating the dining area from the bathroom. Hot water travels the shortest possible distance to reach the bathroom through a highly efficient installation.

The distribution in this home is opposite to the norm: the sleeping area is on the ground floor, and the main rooms are on the first floor, thus making the most of available natural light.

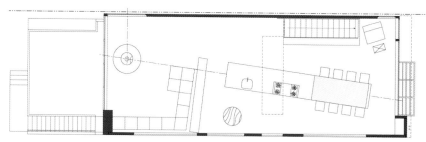

Ground floor

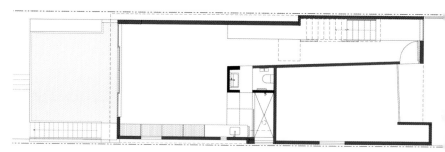

First floor

Light is filtered through to the ground floor bedroom via a huge skylight in the ceiling on the first
floor and then a smaller skylight in the kitchen
floor.

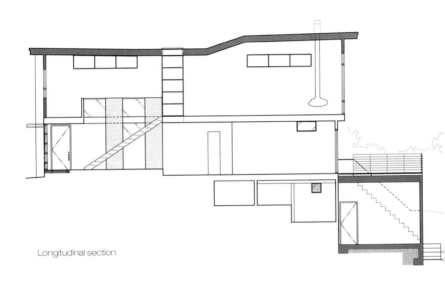

Longitudinal section

A 32.8-foot-long piece of furniture placed diagonally—to optimize space—in the principal living space, stores all the kitchen equipment and also serves as an eating area.

S Home | Linardi, Mercuri, Grundy/ODR

Location: Melbourne, Victoria, Australia | Photos © Derek Swalwell

A spacious area combines the house's main areas, a terrace, a double-height atrium, and a small studio. The outer skin is a succession of aluminum and black-enameled, corrugated metal sheets.

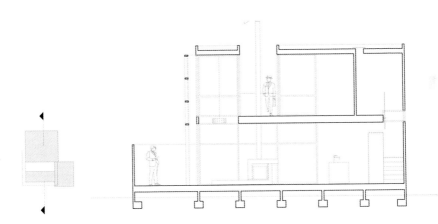

Longitudinal section

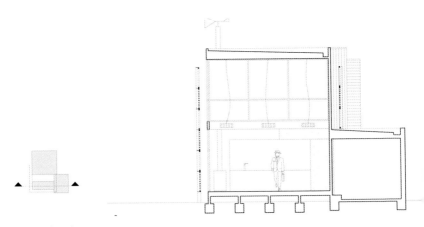

Transversal section

This 19.7 feet high cube solves the problem of limited surface area and expresses itself from the inside outwards, looking out by day and inwards by night when the interior is illuminated like a light box.

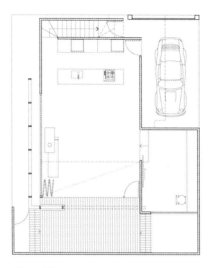

Ground floor

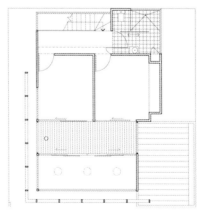

First floor

On the outside, the house has an industrial look, in contrast with the strong colors and plastics used on the inside, as in the bathroom, where fuchsia panels are sure to kick-start anyone's day.

To create a spacious house, the only divisions are moving translucent walls. The highlight is a system of interchangeable moving plywood and polycarbonate panels.

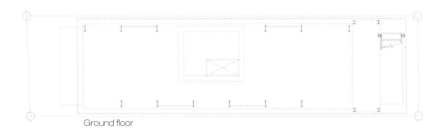

Ground floor

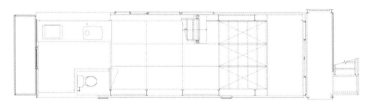

First floor

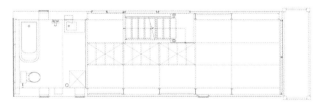

Second floor

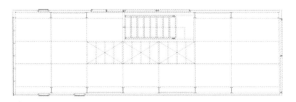

Third floor

The bathroom's simple partitions are made of alveolar polycarbonate, which give this space a distinct feature. These and a system of steel pipes allow the bathroom to blend into the neo-industrial house.

Girona House | Raúl Campderrich Pons/Air Projects

Location: Girona, Spain | Photos © Jordi Miralles

Wooden stairs lead up to a bright living/dining room on the first floor. The panes in the stairwell allow light to flow from here to the upper levels.

First floor

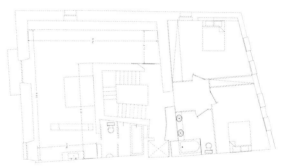

Second floor

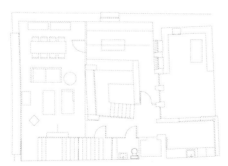

Third floor

A dark-stained concrete partition with a pass-through serves as a separator in the bedroom, while at the same time adding a modern touch to this room. The brown tiling in the bathroom lends sophistication.

One of the most spectacular features of this renovated deluxe duplex is the new double-sided fireplace. Red plaster walls are dramatically set off against the custom-stained dark brown oak floors.

Lower level

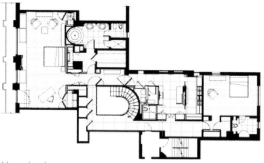

Upper level

An extensive master bedroom is located on the upper floor, where a wide wooden window seat runs along the entire length of the exterior wall, where picture windows offer fantastic views of New York's Central Park.

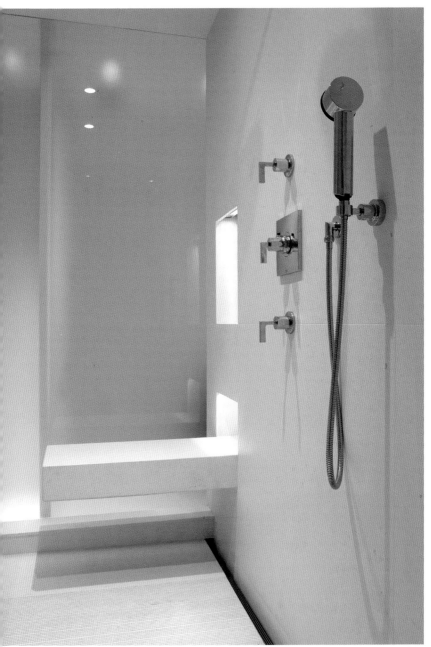

This luxurious private apartment in Parma includes an indoor pool and wine cellar. Using informal and rugged materials, the designers have produced a chic atmosphere.

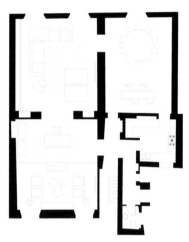

Second floor

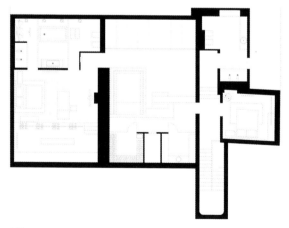

Attic

A 'tattoo-painting' was applied in the bedroom and 'piecing' in the living room. This apartment is the reflection of its owner's lifestyle: a young man leading a modern life in an ancient space.

Dark colors, black floors, and gray walls create an elegant home as well as a strong contrast between the original, historical building and the refurbished apartment interior.

The same materials have been used throughout the project, but in different configurations: black Brazilian stone was used for the fireplace, as well as for the bathroom floors, walls, basin, and bathtub.

Apartment Lidingoe | Medvind Architekter

Location: Stockholm, Sweden | Photos © Åke E:son Lindman

Overlooking Frihammen harbor, this apartment is situated on a steep hill, sloping down toward the Baltic Sea. The master bedroom's walls and ceiling are covered in Merbau wood.

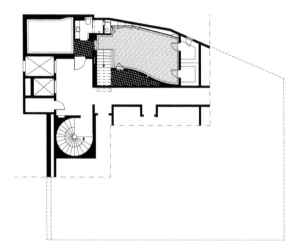

Basement

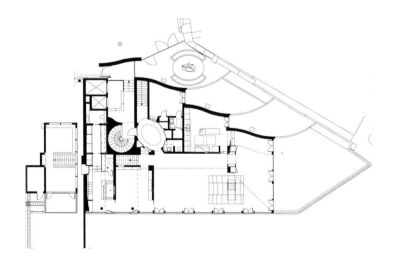

First floor

Basalt floors, rough-cut slate walls, and walls painted with marble stucco combine with subtle lighting to create a tranquil bathroom, ideal for bathing and grooming in peace.

West Village Loft | Abigail J. Shachat/AJS Designs

Location: New York, NY, USA | Photos © Björg Magnea

To create a space that feels more expansive, the wall separating the living areas from the master suite was removed, thus opening up the southern window wall and flooding the space with daylight.

Floor plan

The materials in this NY loft were chosen for their depth, warmth and durability. One of the bathrooms is covered, floor to ceiling, with cork, which envelop the occupant.

Family Duplex | Cristobal Lucea, Xavier Portillo

Location: Baix Llobregat, Spain | Photos © Miquel Tres

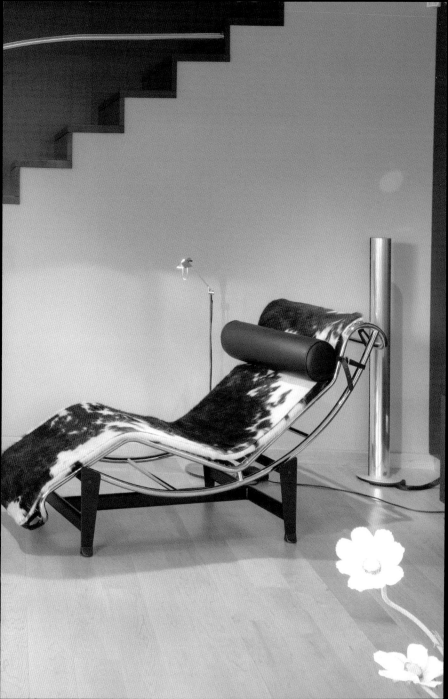

The main aim of this 3,229-square-foot duplex in the old quarter of a coastal town was to create open spaces and make the most of available daylight. The designers created large areas so the owners have room to entertain.

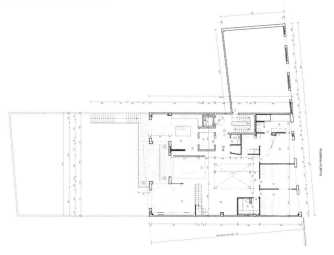

Ground floor

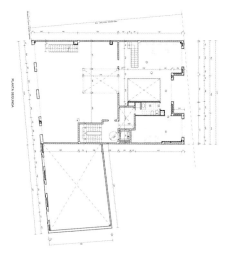

First floor

Most of the doors were eliminated to create a visually fluid space. All rooms are situated around a light shaft in the middle of the home.

As in the rest of the house, the walls of the master bedroom, bathroom, and individual dressing rooms are covered in sophisticated wengue wood, visually uniting these three rooms.

Pied-à-terre Apartment | Bonetti Kozerski Studio

Location: New York, NY, USA | Photos © Matteo Piazza

The pied-à-terre apartment is located within the
Time-Warner Center at Columbus Circle and was
redesigned for a European couple.

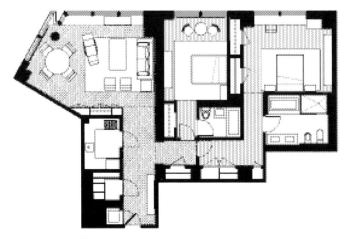

Floor plan

Overlooking the Hudson River, this apartment receives plenty of bright light from the west, which the designers chose to subdue by staining the floors and adding paneling made of Sucupira, a Brazilian tropical hardwood.

Ray 1 | Delugan Meissl Associated Architects

Location: Vienna, Austria | Photos © Hertha Hurnaus

Ray 1 is situated on the flat roof of a 1960s building in a residential district. The interior space is designed as a loft with various functional areas, which are defined by different floor levels.

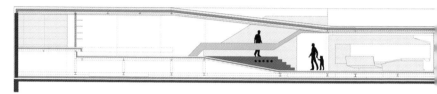

Longitudinal section

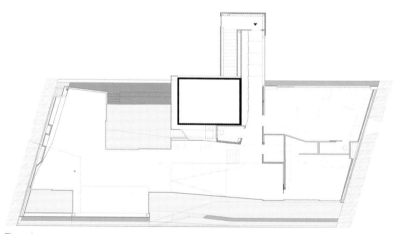

Floor plan

The spacious living area and open kitchen are raised almost a meter above the bedrooms. The centrally located kitchen acts as a transition point between the living and sleeping zones.

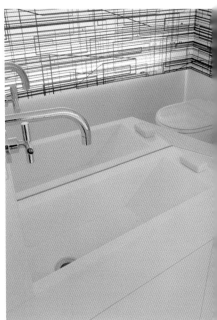

The white minimalist bathroom and bedroom have an almost futuristic feel. The continuity between the exterior and interior is also notable in the shape of the furniture.

A steel, glass, and wood switchback staircase is cantilevered off the mezzanine level and connects the two levels of this penthouse loft. Custom bamboo steps match the flooring.

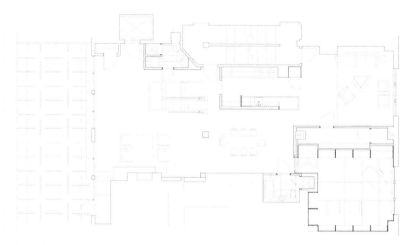

Lower level

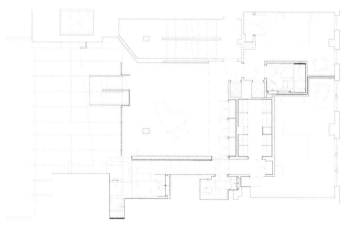

Upper level

With views of Tribeca streets below and Manhattan's city lights beyond, bathing in this urban loft must be a truly unique and luxurious experience.

A central rotating media column in this rooftop apartment incorporates a number of technological devices for entertainment, information, and communication.

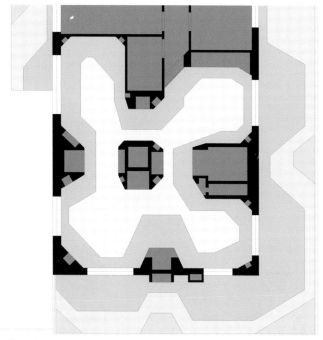

Floorplan

ROTOR is a "protoprogrammatical" penthouse that dissolves traditional spaces, combining new media, technological effects, and sense-stimulating elements such as sound patterns and light pulses in a "dynamic space continuum," according to the architects.

Two shoebox-size apartments in Greenwich Village were transformed into two generous spaces thanks to flexible interior design solutions, including custom-designed furniture.

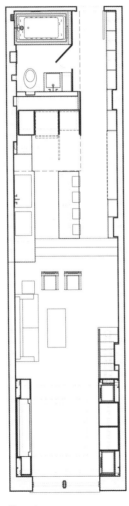
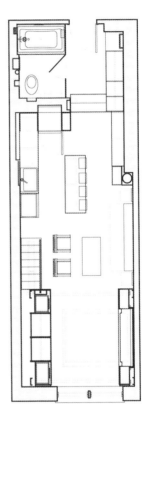

Floor plans

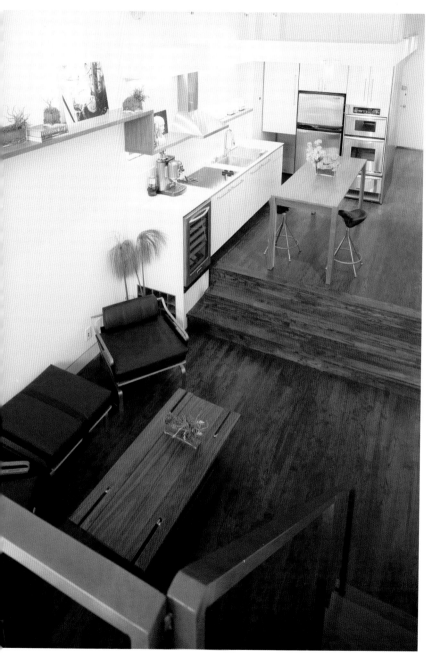

A high-tech kitchen reveals all kinds of surprising nooks to store dishes or wine, for example. A top-loading dishwasher doubles as a second sink. All at the push of a button.

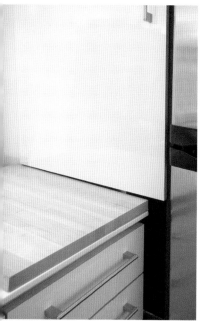

City Lounge | Johannes Will

Location: Vienna, Austria | Photos © Hertha Hurnaus

The main walls of this apartment have been dismantled. There are doorways without doors between the bathroom and kitchen areas, and a large unit with oblique shelves divides the living and working areas.

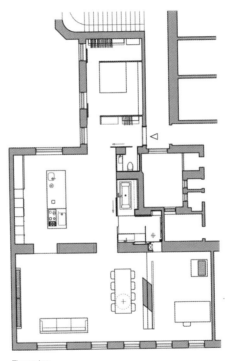

Floor plan

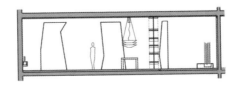

Section

Resin panels replace customary tiles in the transparent bathroom. Living is reduced to its essentials in this apartment, creating an interesting play of light, shadows, and materials.

Vilassar Apartment | Agustí Costa, Estudi de Disseny

Location: Vilassar, Spain | Photos © David Cardelús

This 764.2-square-foot apartment was remodeled to accommodate a young couple without children and with limited financial resources, who, nonetheless, appreciate good, practical design.

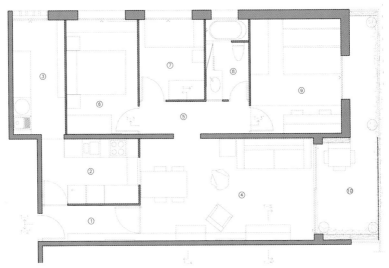

Floor plan

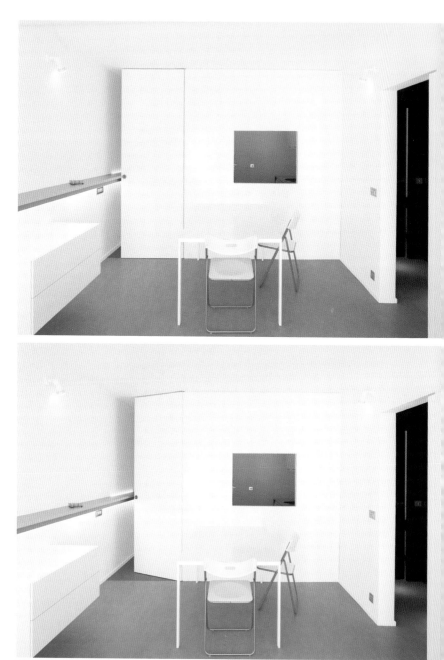

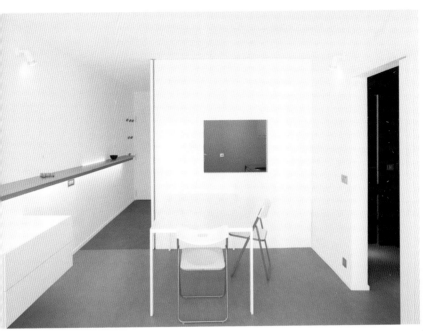

The space was divided in a typically 1970s way, with lots of closed rooms. Now, the main room is one open space, including the entrance hall and kitchen which can be closed off when needed.

The bathroom was radically changed: the tiles were removed and the water surfaces covered in thick plaster and treated with pool paint. The mirrors interact with the corridor.

Flat in Rue St. Fiacre | P. Harden, Atelier 9 Portes

Location: Paris, France | Photos © Philippe Harden

A central block in this apartment, located near the grand boulevards of Paris, divides the main living area from the private areas. Inside the block is a bathroom and dressing room.

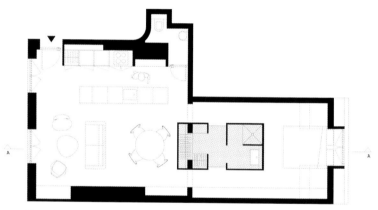

Floor plan

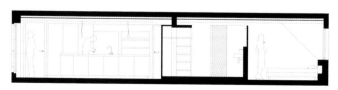

Section

The walls and ceilings have been painted in white allowing the original tile flooring, which was restored, to stand out, creating a lively graphic effect.

Flat in Castiglioni | Studio Rodighiero Associati

Location: Mantova, Italy | Photos © Antonio de Luca, Alessandro Lui

The traditionally private areas, such as those for sleeping, cooking and washing are defined by free-standing cubes, which filter and shield other social activities.

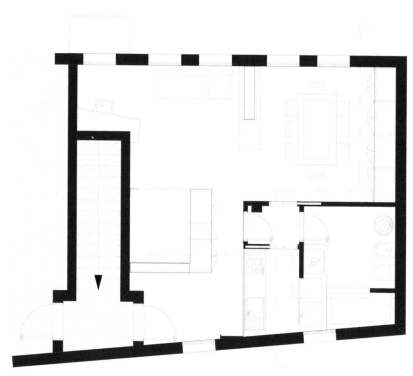

Floor plan

The movable objects provide flexibility. Large-scale images printed on 3M films on the kitchen/bathroom cube give the feeling of stepping out into a black-and-white forest.

The flat is designed for a young couple who love design and dance. The bedroom is shielded from all other social activities, such as eating, studying, and entertaining.

Apartment in Paris | Peter Tyberghyen

Location: Paris, France | Photos © Alejandro Bahamón

This luxurious apartment uses color and almost invisible furniture to make the most of a small space. Colored mosaic tiles define different spaces.

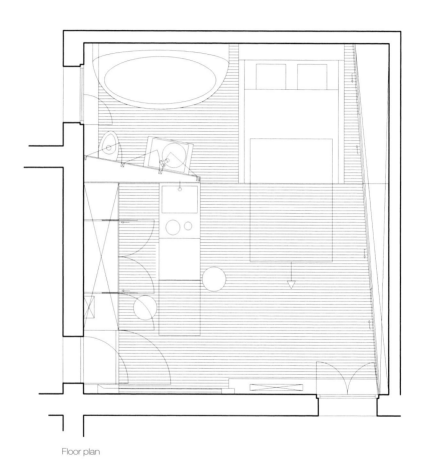

Floor plan

Studio in Melbourne | Six Degrees Architects

Location: Melbourne, Victoria, Australia | Photos © Shania Shegedyn

The design of this studio is carefully planned to allow freedom of movement. Each space is visually separated by different flooring, such as polished cement, wooden planks, and mosaic tiles.

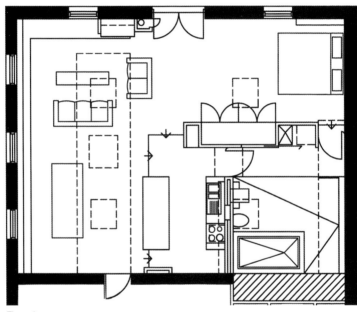

Floor plan

The decor of this nearly square-shaped studio—
a combination of gray tones with luminous white
walls—adds a characteristic feature to this home
and gives it visual continuity.

The bathroom has no door, but the tall gray structure separating the bedroom from the kitchen also helps preserve the bathroom's privacy.

All the furniture in the living room is made of cast bronze and was designed by RPLG studio. The large open space of this London home with industrial parquet flooring lets in plenty of daylight.

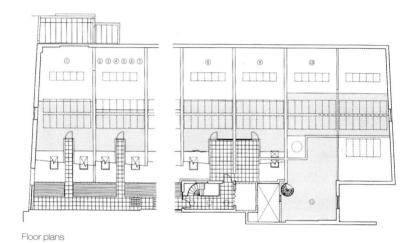

Floor plans

Subtle lighting provides the required ambience in each room. Meanwhile, during the day, enormous skylights illuminate the entire studio.

There were a number of difficulties in the interior design of this flat, which were solved with a bag of tricks. The architects experimented with the use of platforms, interactive furniture, and sculptural ceiling work.

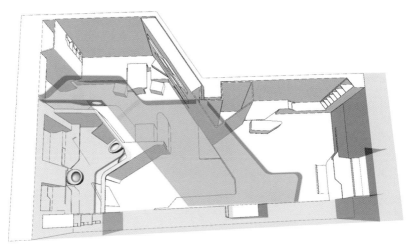

Perspective

Nearly all the furniture was custom designed to transform and adapt the space in different ways. Floor, seating, and sleeping spaces double as storage areas.

Volcanic rock is used in the shower, adding a modern touch to the bathroom. The light sculptural ceiling of the main space continues through to this room.

This small apartment on the Belgian coast is a work of carpentry genius, consisting of a cupboard and a table. The cupboard incorporates the bedroom while the table makes up the kitchen.

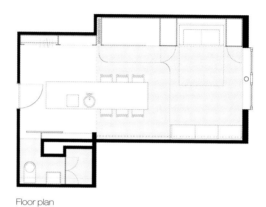

Floor plan

Section

A sliding door opens onto a small, yet functional bathroom, while at the same time hiding shelves behind the kitchen table to store necessary kitchen utensils and provisions.

All in One Piece | Beriot Bernardini

Location: Madrid, Spain | Photos © Ángel Luis Baltanás

A mezzanine created above the entrance adds an extra 86 square feet to this 290.6 square-foot apartment. The wooden structure neatly packs in storage and sleeping areas. The stairs roll out to reveal a closet.

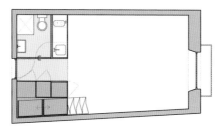

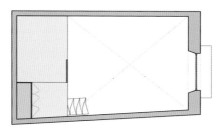

Floor plans

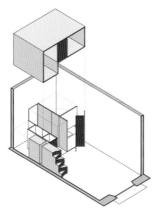

Exploded view

Section

There is storage space and a bathroom in the bottom half of the structure and a 4.92-foot-high bedroom on the upper level. The kitchen is hidden behind a panel of folding doors.

Optibo | White Architects AB, White Design

Location: Gothenburg, Sweden | Photos © Richard Lindor, Bert Leandersson

Optibo is a three-room flat in an area equivalent to a small one-room flat. Most of the furniture collapses into the floor and can be moved up and down to change the function of the room. Each piece can be adjusted to the user's needs.

Floor plans

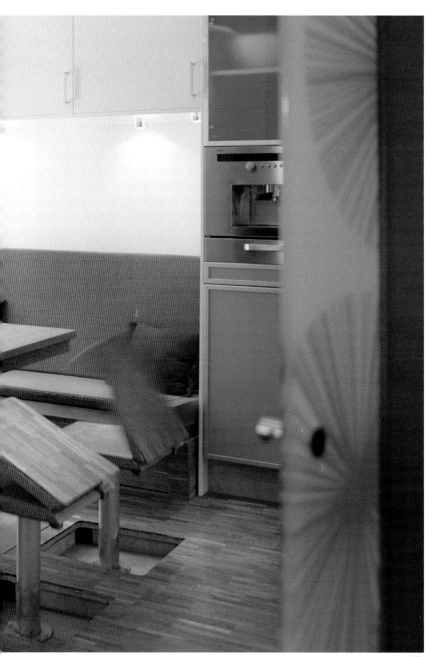

Lighting is very important here, as it allows the character of the flat to be changed accordingly. Energy-efficient and long-life spots are used to emphasize certain parts and details of the flat.

Studio on Madison Avenue | Kar-Hwa Ho

Location: New York, NY, USA | Photos © Björg Magnea

The virtue of this 592-square-foot studio is its height, which is exploited to maximize the available space. A translucent glass panel separates the bedroom from the kitchen and filters through some sunlight.

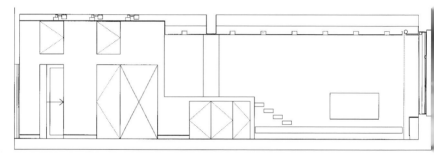

Section

Studio 31 | Geneviève Marginet

Location: Brussels, Belgium | Photos © Vercruysse & Dujardin/OWI

This small flat takes its inspiration from futuristic films from the 1960s and 1970s. A table with rounded edges hides all kitchen utensils and serves as a workspace and dining area.

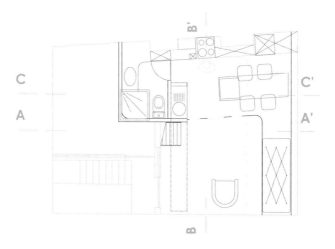

Lower level

Mezzanine level

415

The bedroom is hidden out of view on the upper level above the bathroom capsule and is easily reached by an attic-style metal staircase, which can be folded away.

Lofts

497 Greenwich Street Loft | Zerafa Architecture Studio

Location: New York, NY, USA | Photos © Björg Magnea

A floating island with a 10-foot-long cararra marble top subtly separates the large open kitchen from the main living space. The kitchen features an 8-foot-tall pantry wall of Italian-made cabinets.

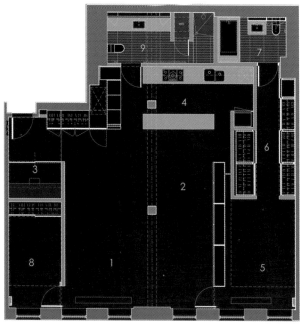

Floor plan

1. Living area
2. Dining area
3. Home office
4. Kitchen
5. Master bedroom
6. Walk-in closet
7. Master bath
8. Bedroom
9. Bathroom/Laundry

The master bedroom is separated from the main living area by a custom walnut cabinet wall. The bathroom interior walls are clad in custom-cut Pietra Cardosa tile with a honed finish.

Carol Austin Loft | Chelsea Atelier Architect

Location: New York, NY, USA | Photos © Björg Magnea

The walls surrounding the kitchen have been eliminated, except the wall separating the kitchen from the bathroom, where colored transparent glass creates a play of light.

Floor plan

Loft for a Young Executive | Brunete Fraccaroli

Location: São Paulo, Brazil | Photos © Tuca Reinés

This loft reflects the taste of a dynamic and modern executive. A rotating plasma television separates the bedroom from the living room and can be viewed from either room.

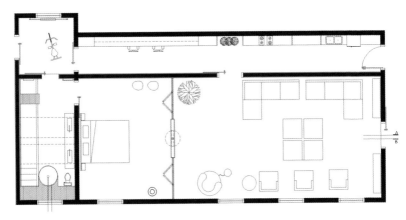

Floor plan

The bathroom with its Japanese ofuro hot tub, multiple mirrors, and warm combination of green accents and wood surfaces converts this area into a place for rest and relaxation.

Tribeca Loft | Gluckman Mayner Architects

Location: New York, NY, USA | Photos © Harry Zernike

Designed to showcase the client's extensive art
collection, this loft is organized around movable
elements that can be repositioned to change the
function of the space.

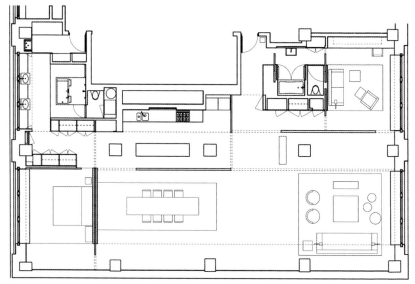

Floor plan

The combination of a variety of sleek modern materials evokes a feeling of efficiency, while the clean straight lines highlight the luxury of a spacious open loft.

Two large aluminum–framed sliding art walls show off the client's work and set the scene for both formal and informal occasions, from entertaining and dining to sleeping and working.

Enclosed in dark brown wood panels, the bathrooms are clad in full-height, back-painted glass, which contrasts with the simple, monochromatic palette of the rest of the loft.

Loft in Madrid | A-Cero

Location: Madrid, Spain | Photos © Santiago Barrio

According to its designers, this is a true loft on account of its location in the center of Madrid, its generous surface space—3,982.4 square feet—and its industrial traits.

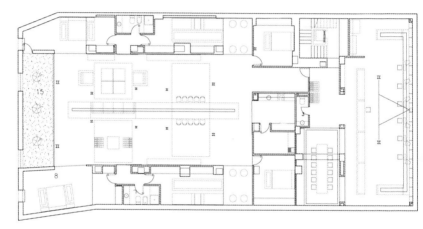

Floor plan

Working around a somewhat chaotic distribution of metal columns, the result is a very elegant and quiet interior in the center of a European capital city.

The distribution of this loft offers great flexibility and fluidity of movement between each of the rooms. The ceilings and walls are covered in plain white acrylic paint.

Putxet Loft | Eduard Samsó

Location: Barcelona, Spain | Photos © Jordi Miralles

Suggestive lines in this 1291.7 square-foot open space indicate the different floor levels. A step-down clearly separates the bedroom from the kitchen and living room.

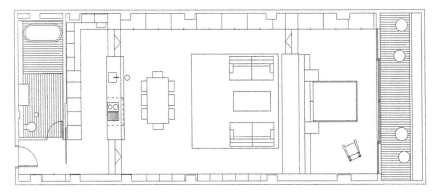

Floor plan

A level down from the living and dining area, the sleeping area faces a small interior courtyard, which gives a feeling of peace and calm that extends all the way to the minimal bathroom at the opposite end of the loft.

This loft was divided into different areas using a variety of materials, levels, and mobile partitions. A glass wall cuts across the loft diagonally and separates the bedroom from the living area.

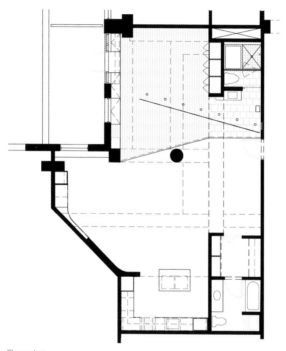

Floor plan

The wood-paneled kitchen integrates with the living area. A rolling counter with rolling cabinets below serves as both food-prep and an informal dining area.

The floors of the living areas are covered in polished concrete, while the master bedroom sits on a wooden platform to create a cozy ambience.

Martins Loft | Toba + Paik, Donn Kermansaarchi

Location: New York, NY, USA | Photos © www.christopherbeane.net

The downstairs of this Sol· lo loft is very minimalist so that the artist can focus on her painting. A floating wall upstairs separates the sleeping area from the washbasin and walk-in shower.

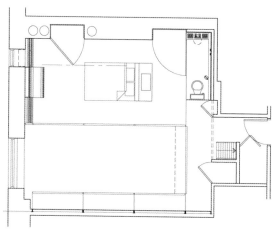

Lower floor plan

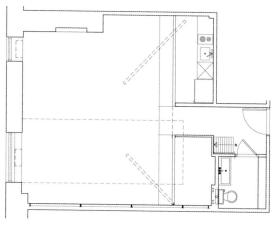

Upper floor plan

The private enclosures on the mezzanine level create a warm, womblike atmosphere and are accesible via steep ship like timber and metal ladder stairs.

360 Loft | SchappacherWhite Ltd

Location: New York, NY, USA | Photos © SchappacherWhite Ltd.

To maximize the use of space, large translucent fiberglass walls and doors are used throughout this urban aerie, filling the place with light while also defining the spaces.

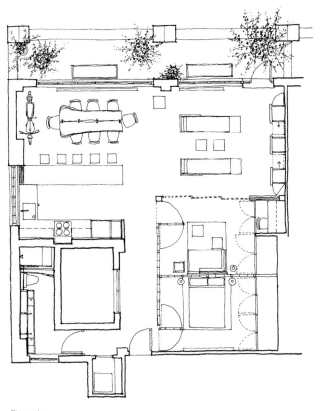

Floor plan

Water in the bathroom travels through stainless steel pipes and is controlled by foot pedals, thus eliminating the need for faucets and leaving a neat surface.

The main challenge of this loft is accommodating living and sleeping areas in the tiny space of 172 square feet, without renouncing comfort. The apartment is accessed from the patio.

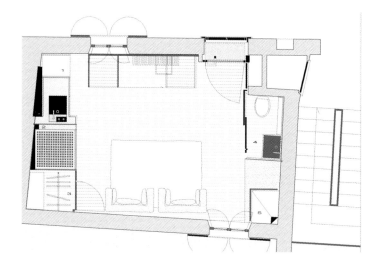

Floor plans

A snug red sofa by day turns into a double bed at night, while other elements such as the shower and closet are revealed when needed by sliding glass panes and doors without handles.

Loftcube | Werner Aisslinger/Studio Aisslinger

Location: Berlin, Germany | Photos © mail@steffen-jaenicke.de

Loftcube is a prefabricated transportable module, with a floor surface area of approximately 430.56 square feet and a variety of design and construction options.

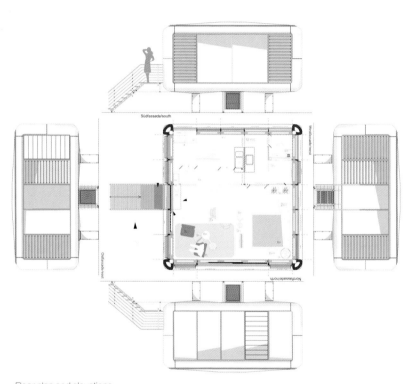

Floor plan and elevations

The inside space is divided by sliding Corian panels on tracks, to which portable furniture modules are affixed. Corian, a durable and easily moldable material, is also used in the kitchen area.

A shared faucet is attached to the panel separating the kitchen from the bathroom, and the showerhead in the bathroom can be used to water the small indoor garden.

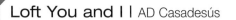

Loft You and I | AD Casadesús

Location: Barcelona, Spain | Photos © AD Casadesús

- anar al cine | - anar al gimnàs
- menjar "xuxes" | - menjar verdures
- mirar la tele | fruita, peix,
- ar de compres | llegums cereals.
- evar-me tard | - fer la compra
- fumar i beure | - anar de vacances
- fer el "vago" | - arribar puntual
| a la feina

The basic idea in this 1,400-square-foot loft is that two people need to live and work in the same space. The design plays with duality, with the idea of you and I, and of living and working.

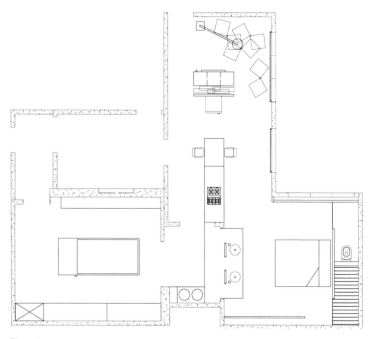

Floor plan

507

The kitchen is the central point here. It opens and connects spaces and ties tying the whole loft together. The coal burner found in the original building was maintained and used as a work area.

Prohibido estacionar.

This studio is very simple and geometrical, using materials such as concrete, marble and steel to give a solid feel and wood to endow the home with a warm and comfortable environment.

Building in Calafell | Maria Almirall/Arquetipus

Location: Calafell, Spain | Photos © Lluis Gené, Ramón Robusté

Incorporating natural light in this initially very dark space and maintaining the original structure, were the main priorities in the conversion of this 13th century building into a family home.

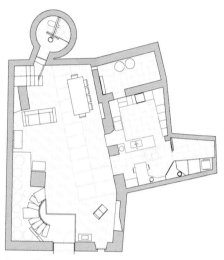

Ground floor

First floor

Elements and materials of the past coexist with modern systems and materials. Glass panels act as both flooring and windows into the past, revealing centuries-old elements of the original structure.

The exposure of existing elements continues to the first floor where the bedroom, study, and simple bathroom—separated by a triangular-shaped dividing wall—are located in an open-plan layout.

The nocturnal area is 'sandwiched' between the living room and the kitchen-dining room. Existing floors were replaced by steel and wood flooring, with metal grating which let in natural light.

Floor plans

527

Satin-glass partitions are an elegant way of
separating the bathroom from the bedroom and
give a certain feeling of expansion in spaces of
reduced dimensions.

Dimuro Residence | Tang Kawasaki Studio

Location: New York, NY, USA | Photos © Andrea Morini

Located in a former caviar warehouse in Tribeca, this 2,500 square-foot loft was totally renovated to house a young family of four. Ceilings were stripped down to the beams, subfloors leveled, and brick walls blasted.

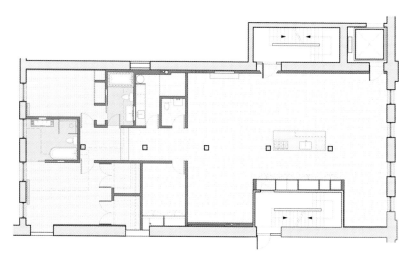

Floor plan

A 14-foot-long fiber-concrete island worktop sits in the middle of the living spaces. The kitchen is concealed behind glossy white lacquered doors.

The Brazilian walnut floors and heavy-timber ceiling are balanced by a framework of white-washed vertical surfaces. There is a dining nook in the place of the former freight-elevator shaftway.

Florence Residence | The Lawrence Group Architects Inc.

Location: New York, NY, USA | Photos © Frank Oudeman

A traditional New York apartment was converted
into a loft for living and working. The living, dining,
and kitchen areas and the bedrooms overlap
and coexist in a combined space.

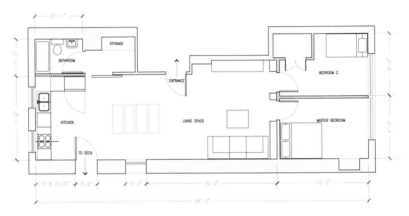

Floor plan

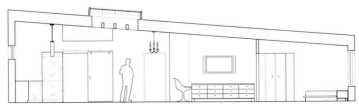

Section

Loft in São Paulo | Brunete Fraccaroli

Location: São Paulo, Brazil | Photos © João Ribeiro

The original structure of columns and iron beams was maintained, as were the original brick walls, complemented by bright-colored tempered-glass panels engraved with designs.

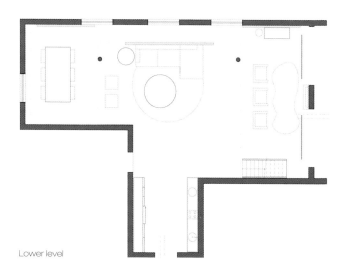

Lower level

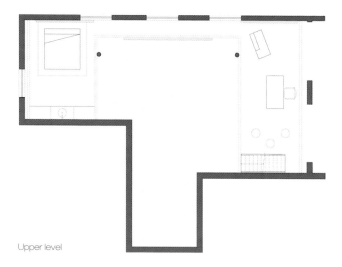

Upper level

The master bedroom and owner-filmmaker's studio are located on a tempered-glass mezzanine, which adds space to the loft and ensures visual continuity between the levels.

Tribeca Loft Apartments | Johan Stylander

Location: New York, NY, USA | Photos © Björg Magnea

These luxurious contemporary loft apartments in a historic Tribeca manufacturing building feature custom kitchens, "frameless" aluminum-and-glass doors, and bathrooms with spa features.

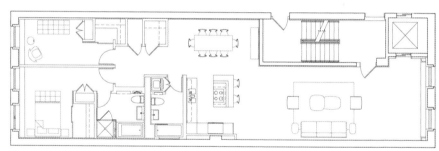

Floor plan

The apartments have programmable recessed and adjusted halogen lighting that includes dim controls. The master and guest bedrooms feature walk-in closets with glass sliding doors.

All bathrooms have stone radiant-heated floors and towel warmers. The master bathrooms have automatic-flush toilets and recessed LCD HDTV.

Loft in Madrid | Manuel Serrano Arquitectos

Location: Madrid, Spain | Photos © J. Latova

This former sculpture workshop has been transformed into an amazingly spacious and luxurious loft on three levels, including an indoor pool on the basement level.

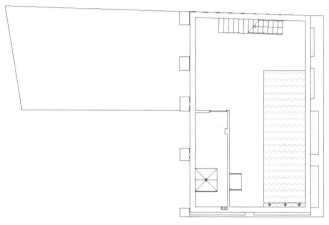

Basement

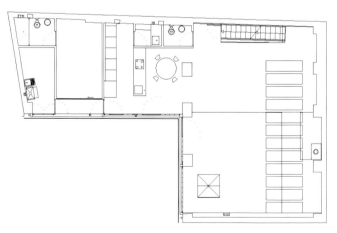

Ground floor

U-glass translucent panels in the roof, on the mezzanine, and in some areas of the floor facilitate the flow of natural light in the apartment.

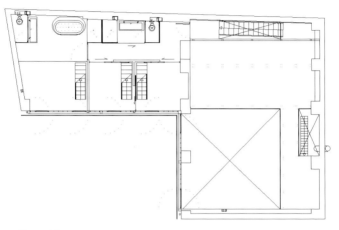

Second floor

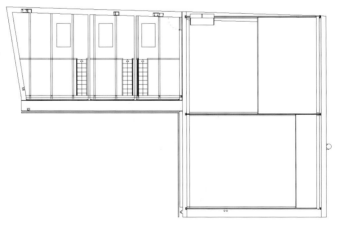

Third floor

Chelsea Loft | Ellen Honingstock

Location: New York, NY, USA | Photos © Björg Magnea

This loft, which housed offices for a textile company, was converted into a comfortable family home with big open living spaces and smaller, cozier bedrooms and children's play areas.

Floor plan

A raised floor hides the plumbing to create a comfortable residential flow, with the bathrooms located near the perimeter of the bedrooms. Lowered ceilings hide mechanical ducts.

Greenwich Village Duplex | Peter Tow/Tow Studios

Location: New York, NY, USA | Photos © Björg Magnea

This one-bedroom duplex is situated in a former commercial garage. The height of the living room has been used to its full advantage. A glass staircase opens onto a double-height living room.

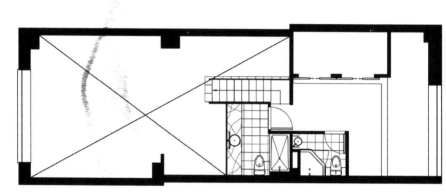

Floor plan

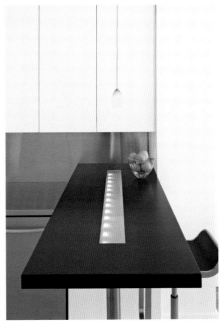

The electrical appliances in this minimalist kitchen are hidden to make the most of the available space. A cantilevered bar separates the kitchen from the living room.

The bedroom and bathroom are reached via the glass staircase. Frosted-glass panes above the kitchen separate the bathroom from the open space below.

Ben Avigdor Lofts | Avi Laiser & Amir Shwarz

Location: Tel Aviv, Israel | Photos © Miri Davidovitch

This former diamond-polishing factory was converted into five differently-size lofts for young professionals. The size of the lofts can be increased or decreased at a later date.

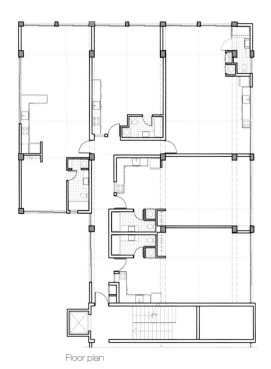

Floor plan

Floors are covered in polished concrete, which gives the lofts a modern touch. Simple furnishings can adapt to the tenants' lifestyle and each functional area is distinguished by a color.

Cooper Square Loft | Desai/Chia Architecture

Location: New York, NY, USA | Photos © Paul Warchol

This former commercial space was converted into a new home for a family of three. The openness of the original space was maintained with private areas fitted in the layout.

Floor plan

Bathrooms and bedrooms hide behind innovative walls of sun-filtering, oblique wooden slats set up in the center of the loft to maintain the original character of the open L-shaped space.

Loft Louise | Jean Leclercq, Anouk van Oordt/uv_a

Location: Brussels, Belgium | Photos © Laurent Brandajs

This former office space was rehabilitated to accommodate an urban loft, maintaining the expansive rectangular footprint. The flooring is dark-stained wenge wood.

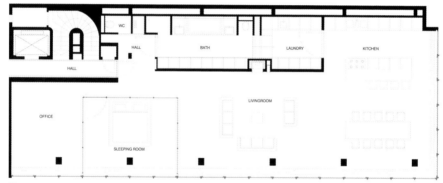

Floor plan

The bedroom is the only enclosed space, surrounded by glass walls that can be transparent or opaque. The architect describes these walls as "luminous, strange, and erotic."

The kitchen and bathroom floors are steel or ceramic tiling. Used in anthracite shades, these materials add a bit of character to an otherwise somber interior.

Wasch Residence | Alden Maddry

Location: New York, NY, USA | Photos © Seong Kwon

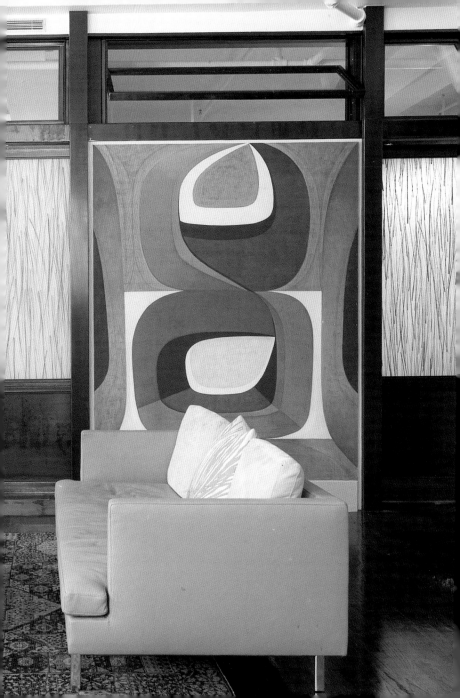

Walls were eliminated to transform this former
hotel and photographic studio. Translucent
sliding panels with resin detailing separate the
bedroom from the living room and kitchen.

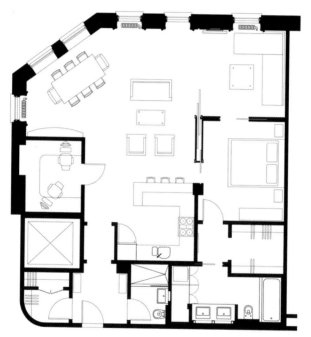

Floor plan

Taking full advantage of the high ceilings, transom windows are used throughout the apartment to improve the circulation of air and maximize available light.

Block of Lofts | Kerry Joyce Associates

Location: Los Angeles, CA, USA | Photos © Dominique Vorillon

A former office in the restored LA Gas Company
buildings was converted into three distinctly
styled lofts. Polished concrete and whitened
wood add elegant and modern touches.

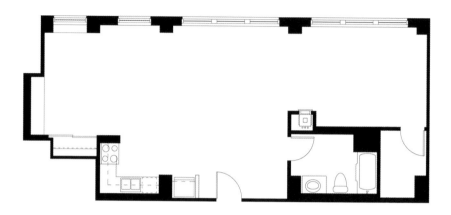

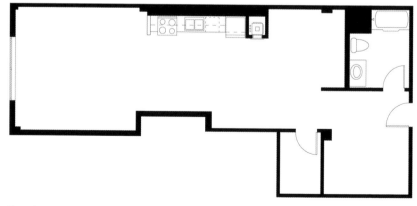

Floor plans

The use of modern furniture in this loft creates a warm and cozy feel to the interior. The distribution of space allows for new areas to be incorporated in otherwise neglected parts.

Brownhill Residence | Gerrard + Tan Architects

Location: New York, NY, USA | Photos © David Joseph

This converted loft makes the most of its large windows and high ceilings and allows the spaces to flow into each other easily. Translucent dividing panels differentiate functional areas.

Floor plan

The consistent use of light-colored wood and translucent glass throughout this New York home, gives the loft a contemporary feel, as well as creating a cozy atmosphere.

The bathroom floors and walls are covered in polished concrete. This material widely used in residential interiors, adds a trendy material to this minimalist bathroom.

Housed in a former department store, this trapezoid-shaped loft belongs to an educational consultant. The kitchen/dining area connects the private with the public space.

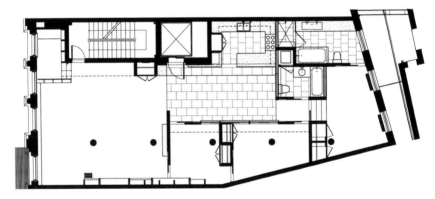

Floor plan

Wood panels, operable sliding glass windows, and wood louvers in the center of the space create a public front—living room and study—for the private back—bedroom and bathrooms.